Keep Yourself Safe

Being Safe
Online

Honor Head

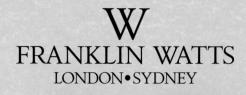

FRANKLIN WATTS
LONDON•SYDNEY

Franklin Watts
First published in Great Britain in 2015 by The Watts Publishing Group

Picture Credits: Cover © damircudic/iStock; 1 © Ilike/Shutterstock; 4 © szefei/Shutterstock; 6 © Shutterstock; 7 © bikeriderlondon/Shutterstock; 8 © © Buenaventuramariano/iStock; 9 © Rmarmion/Dreamstime; 10 © Paul Vasarhelyi/Shutterstock; 11 © gorillaimages/Shuttrstock; 13 © Pamela Moore/iStock; 15 © ClarkandCompany/iStock; 16 © Vesna Andjic/iStock; 16 © J2R/Shutterstock; 18 © Stefano Tinti/Shutterstock; 20 © Hung Chung Chih/Shutterstock; 23 © aleciccotelli/Dollarphotoclub

Series Editor: Eloise Macgregor
Series Designer: Alix Wood
Illustrations: Alix Wood

Dewey number 004.678
HB ISBN 978 1 4451 4428 3
Library ebook ISBN 978 1 4451 4431 3

Printed in China

Franklin Watts
An imprint of
Hachette Children's Group
Part of The Watts Publishing Group
Carmelite House
50 Victoria Embankment
London EC4Y 0DZ

An Hachette UK Company
www.hachette.co.uk

www.franklinwatts.co.uk

Contents

Hi!
I'm Safety Sam.
I'll help you learn
how to be safer
online.

We love being online

Being online is great. You can keep in touch with friends and family, find websites to help with your homework and research your favourite things.

You can use your computer, mobile or tablet to get online to share stuff and to join new internet groups and chatlines. But you should never buy things or do shopping online unless you have an adult with you.

It is easy to give away lots of information about yourself to people you chat with online, but if you can't see them, how do you know who they really are?

Ask Safety Sam

Why do we need to keep safe online?

- Some people pretend to be someone they are not for bad reasons.

- Sometimes people **bully** other users.

- You might see things that will upset you.

Keep it private

It is important to keep some things about yourself private when you are online. Be smart about what you say.

Never tell anyone you meet online your address, age, telephone number, where you play or go to school. Don't give them any information about your friends or family.

BEWARE

Choose a **username** for when you are online, not your real name. Use a nickname when gaming or in a chatroom.

If someone wants to chat about something that is personal or embarrassing, be polite but say you don't want to talk about that. If they won't stop or start being rude or nasty, leave the site, tell an adult and report it online.

Ask Safety Sam

What should you do if someone asks you questions that you shouldn't answer?

- Leave the webite at once.
- Tell a **trusted adult**.
- Don't worry if that seems rude. They shouldn't have asked you!

Smart passwords

To help keep your online stuff private, take some time to think of a really good password. If someone finds out your password, change it.

Your password should be a mix of letters and numbers. Don't use a birthday or your pet's name. Try and think of a password you'll be able to remember without writing it down.

1pizza2chips

Whenever you set up a **profile** always set the **privacy settings** as high as possible. Ask an adult or older brother or sister to help you with this.

Ask Safety Sam

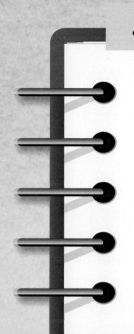

Can I share my password with my best friend?

- No, only tell your parents or carers.
- If your friends ask, say you're not allowed to tell them.
- Don't store your passwords on your computer.

BEWARE

Always **log out** properly when you've finished, especially if you are using a shared computer at school or in the library.

Careful sharing

It's great to share photos and videos with people you know, but be careful. Once a picture or video is online, it can be seen by people you don't know.

Would you be happy for strangers to look at some of the pictures you share with your friends? A picture might be funny to you and people you know, but it might be embarrassing if a stranger saw it.

Something you put online can give away a lot of information about you. What would a stranger find out about this boy if he put this photo online?

BEWARE

Only post holiday photos online when you're back home. Otherwise criminals might see them and realise your family is away and the house is empty.

Ask Safety Sam

How can I make sure I share carefully?

- Check with other people in the photo that they're happy for it to go online.

- Show your family. They might spot something that you haven't.

- Don't put a photo online that you wouldn't want your parents or teachers to see.

Making new friends

Online is a great place to join **forums**, message boards, games and chat about your favourite things. But some people don't tell the truth online.

There could be older people online pretending to be someone your age. These people could be dangerous. Most people online want to be friendly and have fun, but some could say nasty or upsetting things.

Hi, we met online!

BEWARE

Never, ever agree to meet anyone you have met online. If someone asks to meet you, say no and tell an adult.

Check out new chat rooms, games and forums with someone older you trust. Look for sites that have a **moderator** and somewhere to **report abuse**.

Ask Safety Sam

Is video chat safe?

- Only with people you know really well.

- Don't video chat with someone you have only met online.

- It's not rude to say no if someone you don't know asks to video chat. They should respect your decision.

Cyberbullying

Posting nasty comments, calling people names, deliberately not letting someone join a game or chat to be spiteful; this is all cyberbullying.

Cyberbullying can happen on computers, tablets and mobiles. It can happen to anyone. If it happens to you, don't be embarrassed or afraid to tell a trusted adult.

BEWARE

If someone starts to cyberbully you, don't answer back. This may make them do it even more.

Report Abuse

Most sites have a 'report abuse' button. Use this if someone is being nasty to you or scaring you. **Block** the person from being able to contact you and tell an adult.

Ask Safety Sam

My friends are being mean to a boy online. What should I do?

- Don't join in.

- Talk to your friends. Maybe they don't realise how upsetting their comments are.

- If you think it's serious, tell an adult.

Choosing websites

There are great websites that will help you with homework or to find out more about your hobby or favourite author, but be careful what you look at.

If you open a website that has something scary, rude or upsetting, close it straight away. Search for a website you need with an adult or older brother or sister.

Ask Safety Sam

How can I find a safe website?

- Try a child friendly **search engine** such as gogooligans and http://primaryschoolict. com.

- Suggest your class puts together their Top Ten Best Websites.

- Add websites you know and like to your **Favourites**.

BEWARE

Some websites offer free goodies to download. Ask an adult to take a look so you don't download something that will damage your computer.

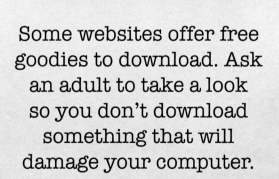

Not everything you read on the internet is true. Ask your teacher to suggest websites or a book for your homework that will give you the right information you need.

Games

Online games are fun to play and help you to learn about stuff as well. Only play games from sites that you know or that friends have played.

Some sites ask you to fill in a profile form with your personal details before you play — don't. The games company might sell this information to other companies. Use a nickname when playing games.

BEWARE

Some games are free but will ask you to buy extras. Always ask an adult or the bill payer before you say yes to buying anything online.

Buy Credits

Some of the other 'kids' you're playing the game with might really be adults. Don't give your email address or other personal details to gaming friends.

Ask Safety Sam

Is it OK to download free games?

• Some games might say they are free but have hidden costs.

• Not all free games will be suitable for young kids to play.

• Before you download a new game, it's smart to ask an adult to check it out.

Keep safe quiz

Answer these questions to find out how you would stay safe online.

1. What is a smart online password?
   a. Your pet's name
   b. Your birthday
   c. A mix of letters and numbers

2. What should you do if you are being cyberbullied?
   a. Tell the cyberbully to stop
   b. Don't answer back and block the cyberbully
   c. Ask the cyberbully why they're being nasty

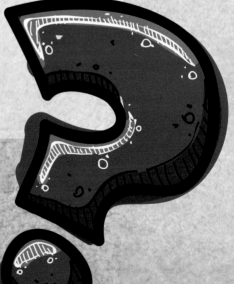

3. If someone you don't know in
   a chatroom keeps asking to meet you,
   what should you do?
   a. Block them and tell an adult
   b. Agree to meet them with a friend
   c. Say you need to get to know them
      better first

4. What's the best way to find
   a safe website?
   a. Just use a search engine
   b. Ask people in a chat room
   c. Ask your teachers and friends

Safety Sam Says

Think about all the
things you can do
online. Why do you
think it's important
to make sure an adult
you trust knows what
you're doing online?

Glossary

block When you stop someone from sending you nasty texts, emails or messages online. Most websites have ways to block people.

bully To say unkind and hurtful things that make people feel scared or upset.

Favourites A place where you can store the addresses of websites you like so you can access them quickly.

forums Places where people can talk to each other and share ideas.

log out Leaving a site. Press the log-out button to make sure that you have shut down the site you were on properly so no one else can get onto it.

moderator A person who checks posts before they go online to make sure they are not nasty or upsetting.

privacy settings Controls on social networking sites that allow you to give permission to who can see your stuff and who can't.

profile Your details for other online users to see. Some people might use their real name and details, other people make up a profile.

report abuse A button that you can press if you are being cyberbullied. The button will take you to a place where you can give the details of what has happened to you.

search engine Website used to find information online.

trusted adult An adult that you know well, who cares for you and would not hurt you, such as a parent, teacher or carer.

username The name you use to log in to sites online. It could be your real name or a made-up one.

Answers from page 20-21
1) c 2) b 3) a 4) c

Further information

Books
Rooney, Anne, *Let's Read and Talk About: Internet Safety*, Franklin Watts, 2014.

Wills, Jeanne, *Chicken Clicking*, Andersen Press, 2015.

Websites
Information on staying safe online and on your mobile
www.safetynetkids.org.uk/personal-safety/staying-safe-online/

CBBC fun quiz on Internet safety
www.bbc.co.uk/cbbc/games/keep-dodge-safe-online

Every effort has been made by the publisher to ensure that these websites contain no inappropriate or offensive material. However, because of the nature of the Internet, it is impossible to guarantee that the content of these sites will not be altered. We strongly advise that Internet access is supervised by a responsible adult.

Index